AF271793

God Forgives

For God did not send His Son into the world to condemn the world, but that the world through Him might be saved. John 3:17 NKJV

For God was in Christ, reconciling the world to himself, no longer counting people's sins against them. And he gave us this wonderful message of reconciliation. 2 Corinthians 5:19 NLT

God wants to forgive you, He wants to blot out *ALL* of your sins. And He is the only **one** who can, so He has made a way to reconcile you to Himself through Jesus Christ and not count your sins against you. He has made provision for you to become sinless, cleansed and righteous. He wants you saved from the consequences of your sins and have you with Him in heaven for all eternity.

He did all that is needed for you to be forgiven and reconciled to Him by hanging Jesus on a cross at Calvary and placing all your sins on Him and then raised Him up from the dead to confirm that He has forgiven you and wiped away your condemnation. He raised Jesus to show you He will raise you up to eternal life too.

To receive His forgiveness He says you must believe and have faith that in the death of Jesus, He bore your sin and guilt and in His resurrection, He forgives and raises you to a new life in Christ Jesus and to eternal life in heaven.

Believe in what God has done for you in Jesus Christ, accept His gift of love and life and you will be saved now and inherit life eternal.

What People have to say about ONE!

This book gives simple and practical steps for individuals and churches to effectively share the gospel. I strongly believe that if the steps outlined in this book are carefully followed, we will be effective in bringing individuals to the saving knowledge of Christ and in turn transform our world with the gospel of our Lord Jesus Christ.

Segun MOTAYO - CAPRO Missionary

The "One!" initiative is an excellent idea - easy to understand process, that is also practicable. The Lord bless you for listening to, and yielding to the Holy Spirit for this brilliant evangelism strategy. I pray the "One!" as an evangelism blueprint will greatly prosper In the hands of the Church for the glory of God, & expansion of His kingdom. Beautiful work!

John. A. EWEJE - Director of Foreign Missions-Foursquare Gospel church in Nigeria.

What a great reminder about our number one responsibility as a believer. One of the world's greatest crimes is not reaching out to lost souls. At a time when sophistication and exigencies of life have made evangelism a bit complex, Brother Tunji has provided us with a simple to follow ABC guide to launch out into the deep. Jesus has no other way to save the world except through us. Following the five steps in One! prayerfully would help us to launch out. Jesus has a prayer request : Matthew 9:38 NKJV [38] Therefore pray the Lord of the harvest to send out laborers into His harvest." You and I can use these five steps to fulfil this divine purpose.

Dr. Wole Olomola - Australia

Copyright 2019: Adetunji Adebakin
All rights reserved. No portion of this book may be
reproduced in any form without the written permission of the
publisher, with the exception of brief reviews.

Scripture quotations marked **NKJV are** taken from the New
King James Version®. Copyright © 1982 by Thomas Nelson.
Used by permission. All rights reserved.

Scripture quotations marked **(NLT)** are taken from the Holy
Bible, New Living Translation, copyright ©1996, 2004, 2015
by Tyndale House Foundation. Used by permission of
Tyndale House Publishers, Inc., Carol Stream, Illinois 60188.
All rights reserved.

Scripture quotations marked **(AMP)** are taken from the
Amplified Bible, Copyright © 1954, 1958, 1962, 1964, 1965,
1987 by The Lockman Foundation. Used by permission.

Scripture quotations marked **(NIV)** are taken from the Holy
Bible, New International Version®, NIV®. Copyright ©
1973, 1978, 1984, 2011 by Biblica, Inc.™ Used by
permission of Zondervan. All rights reserved
worldwide. www.zondervan.comThe "NIV" and "New
International Version" are trademarks registered in the
United States Patent and Trademark Office by Biblica, Inc.™

yesheis is an interactive online platform to help you search, discover and share the gospel online, delivered to guests and Registered Users through both website and mobile applications. Find out more at www.yesheis.com

YouVersion and its contents, features and functionality (including but not limited to all information, software, text, displays, images, video and audio, and the design, selection, and arrangement of the same), are owned by Life.Church. Find out more at www.bible.com

ACKNOWLEDGMENTS

This guide is an inspiration.

A Sunday morning inspiration, and to be precise- a June, 1st, 2019 Sunday.

He started with one word - ONE! and in the 10 odd minutes that followed during a Sunday morning service in Lagos, Nigeria, He filled my conscious mind with shades of ONE! I wrote as fast as my mind could process and these are the five steps I condensed.

Consequently, God deserves all the credit.

He inspired the writing of ONE! with Himself.

All the credit and glory is due to You, and I gladly give it to the greatest ONE!

Two others have influenced me greatly- Max Lucado whose writings and messages bless and inspire me and Remi Lawanson Ph.D. who guided me into evangelism as a practical expression of loving God. To them both, I am also deeply grateful.

Lastly, to the many many teenagers who have passed through Teens Church, Foursquare Gospel Church, Yaba, Lagos, since 2000, thank you for open hearts and the opportunity to love and nurture. You all have inspired me to no end.

FORWARD

The world in which we live today is inhabited by over seven billion people. Of these, 2.4 billion (29.8%) are Christians; 1.9 billion (24.6%) are Muslims; Atheists 1.2 billion; Hindu 1.1 billion; Budhists 1.2 billion; Chinese traditional religion 394 million. The statistics for Christians include Non-Pentecostals. What a burgeoning population! Yet science tells us that amazingly, our fingerprints differ one from another. The fact that no two individuals are exactly the same points to us the picture of a God who is particularly interested in the individual lives and who has plan for each person.

Two inferences in the Bible which clearly explain the importance or value God attach to us as individual souls is Matthew 16:26 which says, *"For what is a man profited, if he shall gain the whole world, and lose his own soul? or what shall a man give in exchange for his soul?"* and the parable of the Lost Sheep recorded in Luke 15:1-7.

In the Lost Sheep narration as given by Jesus Christ, one sheep went astray out of the hundred in the shepherd's fold. The shepherd left the ninety nine and went in search of the one that was missing. On finding the lost sheep, he called friends and neighbors to rejoice with Him. The lesson here is that God places high premium on us individually as His creation. Jesus Christ is the Good Shepherd who gave His life as a ransom for all. A soul is indeed precious to God and that is why He sent His Only Begotten Son, Jesus Christ to die for our sins so that all will come under His reign.

No wonder Jesus said in Luke 15:10, *"Likewise, I say unto you, there is joy in the presence of the angels of God over one sinner that repenteth."* He had earlier said in verse 7, *"I say unto you, that likewise joy shall be in heaven over one sinner that repenteth, more than over ninety and nine just persons, which need no repentance."*

Have you imagined what it means to be without Christ and for such a person to spend eternity in the torment of hell? That is why we must wake up as Christians and rescue the perishing. The most important mission and assignment Jesus Christ committed into our hand before His ascension is evangelism and soul-winning - Matthew 28:18-20; Mark 16:15,16. Go and make disciples of all nations is a worldwide mandate of Christ to the Church. Consistent obedience to the mandate is crucial to the second coming of Christ - Matthew 24:14.

This book, ONE! written by our dearly beloved Bro. Tunji Adebakin who has worked with teenagers for over two decades presents evangelism and soul-winning as a task everyone of us as Christians must be involved in by targeting individuals with the message of salvation. The book is a simple, non complex and easy-to-read guide on personal evangelism/soul-winning. It involves five steps: One Name; One Prayer; One Invite; One Soul; One Life.

The process: Identify one name that Jesus died for and who is yet to submit to Jesus' love. Pray one prayer that the Holy Spirit will reach out and convict one sinner. Send a loving and consistent invitation to one invitee to experience Jesus. This the author suggested can be through social media platforms such as facebook, twitter, text message, phone call, email and video. Ensure that one soul which is worth more than everything on earth responds positively to Jesus' call to salvation. Follow up one life that has received the abundant life available in Jesus Christ at a time.

These 5-steps one-goal outlined in this book can be adapted by individual, cluster, group or a church in reaching out to lost souls. Satan will not easily give up on his mission to steal, to kill and to destroy, and that is why we too as Christians must not give up on snatching souls from the clutches of Satan and translate them into the kingdom of God.

Knowing that God has called us all to pursue that which is his heartbeat - evangelism and soul-winning, the five steps practical guide outlined here is a sure and effective strategy to achieve the growth of the church which is a dire need in the Body of Christ today. This book no doubt has the prospect to rekindle the spirit of evangelism in the life of Christians and ignite the fire in our churches.

I commend it to churches, groups, home cells and everyone who desires to see souls saved into the kingdom of God. He that winneth souls is wise and they that turn many to righteousness as the stars forever and ever (Prov. 11:30; Daniel 12:3).

It is my prayer that this book written under the influence of the Holy Spirit will bring blessings to every reader as we look forward to the soon coming of our Lord and Saviour, Jesus Christ.

Rev. Samuel Aboyeji
General Overseer
Foursquare Gospel Church in Nigeria

TABLE OF CONTENTS

ONE!LIFE -Made all the difference!

INTRODUCTION

If you have an active relationship with Jesus, then you are that One!, He went out to look for leaving the ninety-nine (99) behind. He searched far and wide, high and low until He found YOU! (Luke 15: 1-7).

The goal of this guide

Jesus has found you and wants you to share the great news about salvation with others in the power of the Holy Spirit. This guide asks you to depend on the Holy Spirit to help you take 5 practical steps to reach out with the good news about salvation through Jesus Christ.

> Any method of evangelism will work, _IF_ God is in it.
>
> Leonard Ravenhill

The 5-Steps are:

One!Name. Asking God to help you identify another lost One!

One!Prayer. Asking God in prayer to touch and save.

One!Invite. Lovingly inviting One!Name to a relationship with Christ and/or a service/program.

One!Soul. Lovingly going out to bring One!Name to a definite opportunity to experience Jesus.

One!Life. A followup plan where you are looking to help One!Name to establish a daily Bible reading plan, communion prayer habits and regular fellowship with other believers.

This guide is intended to challenge you to be One! who goes after another One! who has strayed away from the Father and Shepherd of our souls. With the help and power of the Spirit of God guiding you through these five steps you will fulfill Matthew 28:18-20 and then encourage and enlist your friends, small groups and church to go after another One! regularly and all year long.

The first ONE! was You.

Then all the tax collectors and the sinners drew near to Him to hear Him. And the Pharisees and scribes complained, saying, "This Man receives sinners and eats with them." So He spoke this parable to them, saying:

"What man of you, having a hundred sheep, if he loses one of them, does not leave the ninety-nine in the wilderness, and go after *the one* which is lost until he finds it? And when he has found *it,* he lays *it* on his shoulders, rejoicing. And when he comes home, he calls together *his* friends and neighbors, saying to them, 'Rejoice with me, for I have found my sheep which was lost!' I say to you that likewise there will be more joy in heaven over *one* sinner who repents.

Luke 15:1 -7 NKJV

JESUS came for You!

The first ONE! was You

The first time you saw him you just knew, you didn't know why, but you knew. Deep down something told you "there is something special about him."

"But he's black Tunde and his eyes droop, don't you like any of these others? Your mum said. 'See, that all-white one is really cute, and look he's smiling.'" You looked at the white one and he came closer and nudged your hand as if to say 'I like you.' You looked at him close up but your heart wandered and you saw the black one out of the corner of your eye and as you looked up your eyes locked – his sad eyes seemed to say "I'm not as good as the others, you better forget me in this lonely corner, besides no one else looks in my direction or considers me as good enough." You felt that tug on your heart again and looked up to your father "can I see the black one in the corner please?"

You left your father's side and crossed the field heading towards the far end where the black short pony huddled alone by himself, passing some of the other ponies (a few came up to give you a friendly nozzle) but you kept your course. When you got to the black one, you stroked his mane, looked into his eyes and wrapped your arms around his neck. You just knew he was the One! for you.

> God loves each of us as if there were only one of us.
>
> Saint Augustine

God in Jesus came after you! He was willing to leave everything else and chase after you. You were the One! for him.

When and Why did God chose you and chase after you?
God decided before the foundation of the earth to adopt us into His own family by bringing us to Himself through Jesus Christ. This is what he wanted to do, and it gave him great pleasure. Consequently, we praise God for His glorious grace and great love that He has lavished on us who belong to his dear Son (Ephesians 1:5-6).

God chose you, you didn't choose Him (John 15:16) so that His grace might be seen and praised now and for all eternity. He chose you for adoption long before the earth was formed. Because it gave Him great pleasure. Not because of anything you had done (You hadn't done anything then).
God chose you because of His great love for you. Ephesians 2:4 (AMP) says, "But God—so rich is He in His mercy! Because of and in order to satisfy the great and wonderful and intense love with which He loved us. "

The extent of God's love for you is captured in Zephaniah 3:17 (NIV) which says, "The Lord your God ...will take great delight in you, He will quiet you with His love, He will rejoice over you with singing."

His focus and love was and is fixed on you. Jesus says in John 15:16 (NIV) "You did not choose me, but I chose you and appointed you so that you might go and bear fruit—fruit that will last—and so that whatever you ask in my name the Father will give you."

You were His One! and now that you are His, He wants you to bear fruit by helping Him to find and bring another One! home to the Father.

Once you realize you have been chosen by God and appointed to bear fruit you are ready for step 1.

One!Name

And she will bring forth a Son, and you shall call His name **JESUS**, for He will save His people from their sins.
Matthew 1:21 NKJV

There is salvation in no one else! God has given no other name under heaven by which we must be saved.
Acts 4:12 NLT

it starts with One!Name.

One!Name.

(A challenge to identify and select One! separated from the Father)

Tolulope was tired and fed up with life, ever since she came to Lagos three years ago things had just gotten worse and worse. She tried to make friends in school but they all seemed to like her for a season and then dumped her for someone else. Even the boys who warmed up to her never stayed for too long. She was tired of been rejected and left out. She decided she was going to look for a church. One Sunday morning, she timidly walked into Sabo Foursquare Teens church completely unknown by anyone. There was a smiling teenager at the entrance welcoming people and smiling warmly she shook her hand and asked her name. Because of that smile, Tolulope went back the following Sunday. As she walked towards the door of the church the same smiling teenager said, 'Hello Tolulope.'

Because the teenager at the door remembered her name, she decided that she was going to come back every Sunday. From then on Tolulope came almost every Sunday for several years before she left for university. The smiling teenager at the door probably had no idea what difference she made by remembering Tolulope's name.

One!Name

Jesus sets before us this amazing challenge: 'As I have loved you, so you must love one another' (John 13:34). Jesus loved us by laying down his life for us. He would still have laid down

His life if it was only for you. He says that you are to follow his pattern and show self-sacrificial love to others too. This should be the mindset of every follower of Jesus, and this guide is intended to help you give it living practical expression.

Jesus says further: 'By this everyone will know that you are my disciples if you love one another' (John 13:35 NIV).

The word 'love' is far more than a feeling or an emotion; it is a conscious decision to treat people the same way Jesus would treat them. (John 12:14–15).The gracious love of God selected you as the focal point of His plan of salvation and searched you out until He found you.

Love is the most effective form of evangelism there is on this planet. Prayerfully selecting One!Name is an act of showing your "love" for someOne! Jesus shows us in John 13:1-5 that love is practical and can be demonstrated by reaching out to people one-by-one.

You can demonstrate this kind of love by selecting One!Name prompted by the Holy Spirit or as you are moved with compassion in your spirit. When you do and follow through you will reflect God's sacrificial love for that person.

What if these questions jump into your mind:

Why should I chose One!Name? And Who should I chose as my One!Name, Friend, Family or maybe Enemy?

Jesus might respond this way, "I chose those who were my enemies and why because I chose to love!"

Jesus is the supreme example of love. He tells us to love God, to love one another (John 13:34-35), to love our neighbor as ourselves and also to love our enemies. During His lifetime He demonstrated love to all those around him and that included Judas who betrayed him, and love for us all by laying down his life.

Jesus chose his enemies, Andrew chose his brother, You and I can choose both and anyone in between too.

The love of Jesus was demonstrated practically by humble caring service. Jesus washed his disciple's feet, he took off His outer clothes and bent down (probably down on His knees) and washed their muddy or dusty feet.

Your first step in this guide is to prayerfully ask God the Holy Spirit to stir you to write below the name of One! who needs to experience a life-changing encounter with Jesus.

One!Name: ....

Then like Jesus did your next step is to get on your knees and **PRAY** for One!Name diligently, desperately, and daily.

One!Prayer.

"Father, Forgive them.." Luke 23:34 AMP

For God so loved the world that He gave His one and only son. John 3:16 NIV

God's Mercy & Grace forgives & saves.

One!Prayer.
(A three-in-One prayer for One!Name)

God inspires prayer, He wills and acts in us according to His good pleasure. He invites you whom He has chosen to pray (Luke 18:1) and to pray constantly about everything. And in particular to pray for those who have strayed away and are lost. God the Holy Spirit helps us to pray aright and helps our weakness in prayer by teaching us what to pray for in line with God's present will. Only the Spirit of God knows the mind of God (1Corinthians 2:11) and so He is the only one who can teach you to pray in accordance with His will.
Also, the Spirit knows the circumstances and mind of the lost soul and is able to speak to the heart the conviction of sin needed to cause repentance (Luke 15:17). Then the Spirit inspires faith for repentance and forgiveness from the Father (Romans 12:3b & Luke 15:18).

We love by giving! God so loved the world, He gave! In this step, you will give by praying! When we learn how to allow the Holy Spirit to pray through us for the lost we will achieve God-sized results. In this step, you will sow seeds of life by praying to God for One!Name to come into a living relationship with Jesus Christ as savior and Lord.
I urge you to pray in line with God's word to God who desires that all men might be saved (1 Timothy 2:4),

I exhort therefore, that, first of all, supplications, prayers, intercessions, and giving of thanks, be made for all men;..For this is good and acceptable in the sight of God our Saviour; Who will have all men to be saved, and to come unto the knowledge of the truth. 1 Timothy 2:1-4.

We ask God who has provided for man's salvation through grace, that is received through faith in Jesus (Ephesians 2:8-9).

While Grace is free (it's a gift from God), it still needs to be accepted. You must stand in the gap and ask God in prayer to shower His gift of grace upon One!Name. Jesus teaches us to ask (in Matthew 7:7), He says ask and you will receive, keep knocking and the door will be opened, keep seeking and you will find) and to be both confident and consistent in approaching God to ask for mercy and grace.

Let us therefore come boldly unto the throne of grace, that we may obtain mercy, and find grace to help in time of need.

Hebrew 4:16

What to ask God to do for One!Name.
There are three focal areas you should ask God to touch in the life of One!Name:

1. Ask for mercy and grace for
One!Name(..)
(Insert name. Print One!Life card for additional names)
Hebrew 4:16-Let us, therefore, come boldly unto the throne of grace, that we may obtain mercy, and find grace to help in time of need.

2. Ask the Holy Spirit to convict of sin.
John 16:8-9 And when He has come, He will convict the world of sin, and of righteousness, and of judgment: of sin, because they do not believe in Me.
Luke 15:18 - I will arise and go to my father, and will say to him, "Father, I have sinned against heaven and before you.

3. Ask for a repentant heart experience and the Spirit to prompt a return to God the Father.
Luke 15:17-18 "But when he came to himself, he said, 'How many of my father's hired servants have bread enough and to spare, and I perish with hunger! I will arise and go to my father and will say to him, "Father, I have sinned against heaven and before you.

Practical prayer must be deliberate, so make quality time to pray and set aside 10-15 minutes each day over the next one week to commit One!Name into God's gracious hands.

Practical prayer will be desperate. David often cried out to God in deep anguish because it was a matter of life and death. Your prayers for One!Name may be the difference between whether he/she comes to life in Jesus Christ or remains in darkness and spiritual death. So pray desperately, someone's life actually depends on you praying.

Practical prayer is consistent, over the next one week pray daily for One!Name and then continue over the next 21 days when you invite One!Name to an outreach program or to attend your church service and until he/she becomes One!Life that God has saved.

To ensure that happens keep him/her in your prayers during the One!Invite and One!Soul steps(which follow right after the One!Prayer step).

Daniel prayed and his prayer was answered on the first day but it was delayed for 21 days by the enemy before the answer arrived. So pray consistently that all obstacles to One!Name accepting Jesus as savior will be removed.

Then you will be ready for the One!Invite step.

One!Invite

For the Son of Man came to seek and save those who are lost." Luke 19:10 NLT

So He says...

"Come and see." They came and saw where He was staying and remained with Him that day. John 1:39 NKJV

Invited to Come & See Jesus!

One!Invite
(A loving and consistent invitation to experience Jesus)

Joy walked passed as if she didn't see Funmi. In her mind, Funmi said "Whaaat ever" "Who cares about you anyway" But before the sentence in her head ended, she felt His presence ease into her thoughts and say, without really saying anything, "She is my daughter too and she's lost. Will you help me point her in the right direction?"

Funmi began to think, "Lord...Do you really expect me to like her, she clearly doesn't like me and may not want to be liked anyway." She hadn't finished the thought when she remembered that just a few months ago she had snubbed Tutu for months before finally accepting to follow her to "The Fellowship". Tutu didn't give up and she always had that smile on her face, even she got no after no. Funmi remembered several times when she had told Tutu "No", "No way, I am busy this week and next week too, for that matter." Even though she wasn't busy at all and in fact had nowhere to go. For some strange reason, Tutu didn't give up. Week after week, after week. It was as if the pleasant smile was plastered to her face and her warm inviting nature couldn't be ruffled by all the sharp NO's she got. It took her three long months of inviting and inviting and inviting.

Funmi glanced at her phone and Tutu's WhatsApp and smiled, the invitation that finally worked was still her DP - Come and See -Jesus. She looked up, Joy was still in sight and only a few meters ahead. She quickened her step, smiled and knew what she had to do, no matter how long it took.

Jesus found Andrew and Peter and He called them to follow him. He made them an invitation that they couldn't resist.

> From that time Jesus began to preach and to say, "Repent, for the kingdom of heaven is at hand."
>
> And Jesus, walking by the Sea of Galilee, saw two brothers, Simon called Peter, and Andrew his brother, casting a net into the sea; for they were fishermen. Then He said to them, "Follow Me, and I will make you fishers of men."
>
> Matt 4:17-19 NKJV

The next step is where you invite One!Name to Come and experience Jesus at a special outreach program; a weekly Sunday Service; or a One-on-One meeting.

Your invitation can take any of the following tracks to get to One!Name:

1. A social media-based invite. It could be a facebook messenger invite, a twitter Direct Message (DM), so long as it goes directly to One!Name and invites him/her to a Jesus experience.

2. A text message, iMessage, or email that also goes to One!Names phone or email.

3. A phone call. A personal and direct phone call to invite.

Using Videos to Invite One!Name

You can in addition to any or all of the three tracks above invite One!Name by share videos using YesHeIs!

YesHeIs is a fantastic App and online platform that I use to invite people to a relationship with Jesus. YesHeIs has amazing video testimonials with a wide array of stories from believers from all sorts of backgrounds and most importantly the videos include an end frame that invites the recipient to accept Jesus Christ. This is crucial for video invites to be effective.

> Now you are ready for the next step - Go out and bring One!Name to a service or outreach program.

One!Soul

And what do you benefit if you gain the whole world but lose your own soul? Is anything worth more than your soul?
Matthew 16:26 NLT

This means that anyone who belongs to Christ has become a new person. The old life is gone; a new life has begun!

And all of this is a gift from God, who brought us back to himself through Christ. And God has given us this task of reconciling people to him. For God was in Christ, reconciling the world to himself, no longer counting people's sins against them. And he gave us this wonderful message of reconciliation.

2 Corinthians 5:17-19 NLT

One Soul is worth more than everything on earth.

One!Soul

(Going out to bring One!Name to experience Jesus)

Jesus came to seek and save the lost because He is Love....
There are several definitions of love, the Greek intonations include
these four:
1. Philia, often translated as friendship or affection
2. Eros, or sexual passion
3. Storge, love of parents, children, and families, and
4. Agape, the love of God for man and man for God.

Agape love is the strongest and purest of the four, but any attempt
to describe agape love will fall far short. For God's love is infinite,
unfailing, immeasurable, eternal and far beyond our human
understanding. God *IS* love. That's what He is. Meaning that's
what He is made of. God's love has been extended to everyone
who has ever walked the face of the earth, whether they believe in
him or not. It didn't matter if they're poor or rich, good or bad,
highly successful or dismal failures, kind or cruel, leaders or
followers.
Nothing we do will make him love us less. And nothing we can try
to do will earn his love. It's a gift and it's free because Jesus paid
the price.
God has loved us from the moment of our conception and will
love us to the day we die, whether we acknowledge Him, scoff at
and disdain Him, deride Him or deny Him. He longs for us to
turn to Him and be born again by His spirit, and to live with Him
forever. So He came down to earth to look for us and to reconcile
and bring us back to the Father.
[Culled from To Everything A Time-YouVersion plan by Eleanor
Watkins & Malcolm Down]

Your goal in this step is to go out in the love and power of the Holy Spirit and bring One!Name to the life-changing love of God through the gospel of Jesus Christ.

Andrew went and found Peter and brought him to Jesus.

> He first found his own brother Simon, and said to him, "We have found the Messiah" (which is translated, the Christ). And he brought him to Jesus. John 1:41-42 NKJV

Often times it will take more than one invitation to get One!Name to attend a church program or service or even a face-to-face, one-on-one appointment/meeting/hang out. The One!Soul step is love in action and involves your going out of your way to bring One!Name to a Jesus experience.

Going out in love to bring One!Name to Jesus

When One!Name accepts your invitation you will want to make sure that he/she actually comes to the program or event. So like Andrew who went to get Peter, you will need to go and get One!Name, that may mean, picking them up from home or school or a cafe that you both know. What is important is that you are willing, (if there is a need) to go out and bring One!Name to attend the service or program that will expose them to the word of life and Jesus.

Consequently, prompted by the Spirit and encouraged by the love of God you show One!Name will attend a program and come into the presence of God. An experience that will deposit the seed of God's word in his/her heart (Matthew 13:1-9).

Lots of people don't give their lives to Jesus the first time they hear the good news. So this may be the first of several One!Name visits to the church or program. Don't give up, don't ever be discouraged if this happens. Almost everyone had to hear the good news several times before they came to accept Jesus into their hearts and became a living soul.

Introducing One!Name to Jesus by sharing your personal testimony.

There will be moments when after you have invited and brought One!Name to a church service or special event that you have the time to talk about the service and the message. This is a great opportunity to share and reinforce the message of salvation using your own personal experience in three relatable steps.

When you have an opportunity to tell your salvation story, what should you say?

Whenever you can, share your personal salvation experience with One!Name using these steps:

1. Talk about what you were like before you got saved.

Identify with One!Name. Share examples of the kind of person you were before you meet Christ and how your lifestyle was flawed and without God. Paul in Acts 21:40 does this when he spoke to the Jews, He deliberately spoke in Aramaic to identify with his audience. He stressed the parts of his life that the listeners could relate with.

Because he was speaking to Jews, he spoke about his Jewish background. You can start by sharing with One!Name about your relatable past. You could drive the conversational to salvation with a comment like "You know, I was ...." or "Did you know, I used to ....".

2. Talk about what happened to you.
It is critically important to talk about what happened to you when you encountered Jesus in concrete terms. The personal details make it real, believable and powerful.

In Acts 22:1-21 Paul gives a very detailed account of what happened to him on the road to Damascus when he encountered Jesus. He heard Jesus' voice. Jesus asked him questions and gave him commands. Paul listened and did as Jesus instructed. Similarly, you could share your personal life-changing encounter and spiritual journey with One!Name. Then lastly.

3. Talk about how you have been transformed.
Flowing from the encounter with Jesus it is important to say in definitive terms how you have been transformed. You should describe the real ways, that Jesus has changed your life for the better. The story of your changed life is living evidence of God's power to change and transform One!Name. Sharing your personal testimony gives you a great opportunity to invite One!Name to a new life in Jesus and you should end your transformation experience with an invitation to One!Name to accept Jesus as savior.

Look forward to a positive response and be ready to lead One!Name into a new life in Jesus and pray a prayer with Romans 10:9-10 as your guide.

> If you confess with your mouth the Lord Jesus and believe in your heart that God has raised Him from the dead, you will be saved. For with the heart one believes unto righteousness, and with the mouth confession is made unto salvation. Romans 10:9-10 NKJV

And with that done and the acceptance of Jesus as savior by One!Name. You are at the final step.

One!Life.

I have come that they may have life, and that they may have *it* more abundantly. John 10:10b NKJV

More abundant life.

One!Life.

(The follow-up plan that shows - God doesn't just love One!Name He loves him unconditionally, Unrepentantly, Passionately & will always love One!Name)

The lioness gives birth to baby cub under the cover of a night lit only by a full African moon, somewhere in Africa's wild wonderful open wilderness. The cub totally dependent on its mother for life and nutrition. The cub will grow up to be the Lion King and ruler of all the jungle but now is a helpless baby cub bounding about unsteadily behind his mother. His mother lovingly licks the cub dry and gently lifts him by the neck and drops him between her protective powerful front paws. Paws with claws that can ripe prey into pieces small enough to feed her cub. Claws that will fight off every predator no matter its size or their number. The lion cub is safe in its mother's embrace and nurtured by her milk. Lionesses are fiercely protective of their cubs and will fight to the death to keep them safe. The cub and Lion King knows it is safe and loved.

God doesn't just love One!Name He loves him/her Personally, Unconditionally, Unrepentantly and Passionately. The revelation that "God loves me" passionately is where the One!Life step starts. This Knowing, Understanding, Believing and lastly Feeling how much and how insanely God loves One!Name and all His children is the start point of the most important relationship of all time and eternity.

The One!Life step is where you follow up One!Name until he/she comes into a personal love relationship with God. This follow-up program encourages a relationship that starts with getting to know and love God through bible reading using a daily reading plan; teaches a regular fellowship time with God in communion prayer and local church attendance.

The One!Life step focuses on your helping One!Name to see and taste the love of God through the word of God by introducing One!Name to a relationship with the Holy Spirit. Finding out about, knowing, and experiencing that love starts in reading and meditating on God's word and is enhanced by prayer. And in particular, the prayer asking for the infilling of the Holy Spirit. Luke 11:13(NKJV) says: "If you then, being evil, know how to give good gifts to your children, how much more will *your* heavenly Father give the Holy Spirit to those who ask Him!" Praying with One!Name to receive the baptism of the Spirit is a key goal of this step.

The Holy Spirit is the teacher who can open One!Name's heart to knowing God through the word. The word of God provides One!Name (and all believers) with the foundation for communion with God in conversation-styled prayer. One of your other goals is to teach One!Name how to turn the Word of God he/she is reading into the keywords for conversational prayer.

A daily bible reading plan
You will likely need to help One!Name to start reading the bible daily. The book of John is a great place to start. It is both encouraging and motivating if both of you read the Word and share your thoughts each day.

Reading the Bible One Chapter at a time with One!Name.
I recommend using the YouVersion bible app to help develop the daily habit of reading the bible alongside with a new believer. YouVersion comes with an exciting and hugely useful feature that allows two or more users to read the bible together from any location and share their experiences, thoughts, and questions in real-time every day.

The [FOOD Challenge One Chapter-A-Day](#) plan is a great one-chapter-a-day plan on John's gospel that you can start with. You will also find many more plans at [YouVersion.](#)

lefined/reading-plans/2428-the-food-challenge-a-chapter-a-day/together/cr... 🔍 ☆

When do you want to start this Plan?

Starting on a future date will give your Friends time to
accept your invitation.

‹   July 2019   ›

Invite Friends

w.bible.com/reading-plans/2428-the-food-challenge-a-chapter-a-day

The F.O.O.D. Challenge - A Chapter A Day

30 Days

This is a 5 step challenge-All you need to do is-READ LISTEN WRITE PRAY and POST. Read-The Word. 1 Chapter-A-Day Everyday. Listen-For God to speak directly to you from a selected verse. Write-make a note/there is a question to help here;. Pray-Say a prayer taken from the Word. Post-Create a verse image and share on Facebook Twitter Instagram Pin it anywhere you like. So Read.Listen.Write-Pray & Post God's word for the next 30 days

PUBLISHER

We would like to thank Adefunyi Alade Adebayo for providing this plan. For more information, please visit
www.itsjustbalance.org

About The Publisher

How do you want to read this Plan?

By Myself
Make your Plan activity private, or allow your Friends to see your Plan activity

With Friends
Invite Friends to join you in this Plan. You'll complete days together at the same pace, and you'll all be able to discuss what God is teaching you along the way.

Praying with your bible open

Praying with the bible open is a simple yet biblical way to develop a daily prayer habit. After reading a chapter of the bible teach One!Name (any new believer can be taught and encouraged this way) to pray by looking closely at one verse at a time and turning the verses that strike his/her heart into a prayer for himself/herself, then family or other needs and concerns. The FOOD Challenge-30 Prayers is a useful plan that combines reading one chapter a day with taking one verse and turning it into a prayer that can start a prayer conversation with God.

Fellowship with Bible-loving believers

Experiencing the love of God will be felt when One!Name fellowships with other believers and experiences worship and the presence of God. Your role is to encourage and ensure that One!Name settles into a bible teaching fellowship of believers and regularly attends Sunday services and mid-week meetings.

This One!Life step is critical to ensuring that One!Name becomes established in the truth and Word of God and grows to maturity so that One!Name can, in turn, follow the 5-Step One!Life guide and bring another One! to Jesus.

Using ONE! as a group [Or as a church]

And He said to them, "Go into all the world and preach the gospel to every creature. He who believes and is baptized will be saved. Mark 16:15-16 NLT

Then the word of God spread, and the number of the disciples multiplied greatly in Jerusalem, and a great many of the priests were obedient to the faith. Acts 6:7 NKJV

Therefore those who were scattered went everywhere preaching the word. Acts 8:4 NKJV

Go and make disciples of all nations.

Using One! as a church growth program

This program will work effectively when small groups, fellowships, and churches use it as an integral part of their outreach plans and drive evangelism through the One! program.

We are planning to use the 5-Step program in our church over a 4 week period, and then with two smaller groups - the youth fellowship and the Men's shortly after. The goal is to reach and bring a minimum of One hundred (100) new converts this year (July 2019 -June 2020) to church and plan to run the One! program every other month as we drive towards our goal.

However, not everyone(group or fellowship) will fit exactly into the time track, expectedly some members will finish earlier and others later and possibly some won't be able to run the full cycle.

Below you will find details of how we plan to run the program monthly, and we suggest you use this timing guide to keep track and give the program a goal and focus. However, you may need to modify it to suit your circumstances or specific upcoming events.

We seek to involve all group and church members, as we run this program along the following suggested 4-week track.

One!Life 4 Week Implementation Track

Week 1:

*Leaders Pray. Pray Fervently!!

*Prepare/print the One!Life 5 step Guide Poster and Pin it up in several strategic notice boards, plan to Share on social when the program launches in week 1.

*Print the One!Life Card, one for everyone in the church (with a condensed 5-step guide on the reverse so it's also a reminder/reference).

*Print the One!Life Wall Poster and plan to pin-it up where members can see it and stick their One!Life cards on it after they have successfully brought One!Name to a church service/outreach program.

* Identify the target church service or program that One!Invite will focus on and print invitations cards for members to use with Social graphics versions too and plan to share in week 2.

* Agree materials to be used for One!Life followup plan. Daily bible reading, for example, can use YouVersion App, so that invited One!Name can read along with the member who invited. Plan to teach members "How to pray with your bible open starting from the book of John so they can share with One!Name how to start a prayer habit. Also, plan how to help new believers find a local fellowship that will provide spiritual cover and growth.

Week 2:

*One!Name & One!Prayer

*__One!Name__ - Introduce and explain the One!Life 5-Step plan and prayerfully ask members to join in.

*Give each member a One!Life Card and ask them to pray to ask God who their first One!Name should be and then fill in that name on the One!Life Card. Give time for those who can't decide on a name immediately.

*__One!Prayer__ - Explain the importance of praying One!Name into God's salvation and explain the three-layered prayers and ask members to plan to commit 10-15 minutes each day for the rest of the week to praying these prayers specifically for the One!Name they have selected and written down. And also daily after that until One!Name comes to Church and experiences Jesus during a service or program.

*Pair members in two's (Jesus sent disciples out in two's)and ask them to agree in prayer with each other the following:

> 1. Pray for each other's One!Name
> 2. Pray for each other to be faithful in praying daily for one week for One!Name and until the end of the month/program.
> 3. When to meet together in church after mid-week service and Sundays to pray for both One!Names.

Week 3:

*One!Invite & One!Soul

One!Invite - Members are prompted to send out Invites during the course of the week across all three options-Social, Text and phone calls. They can also be given printed invitation cards. Several invites may be needed before a confirmation to attend service or program is secured, members are encouraged to keep at it and be politely persistent.

One!Soul - When members secure confirmations then they can accompany or bring One!Name to church for service or program. Some invitees will prefer the safety of being accompanied rather than coming on their own.

Week 4:

***One!Life**

* Prepare to receive selected, prayed for, invited and brought to service visitors who have experienced a life-changing encounter with Jesus.

*Members are reminded about how to begin the followup and discipleship process and are requested to help One!Name to begin to read the bible daily. They can read the bible together one chapter-a-day together using the YouVersion Bible App. This will encourage and help One!Name develop the new habit of daily bible reading and create an accountability partnership for spiritual growth.

Members will also help One!Name to begin to pray with open bible, taking one verse that jumps up to be prayed for self, family, friends, the nation or peculiar situations.

Then lastly, to encourage One!Name to join a fellowship of believers regularly.

When groups- Units in church, Home fellowship Cells, or even entire church locations- pray sincerely to God to help them proclaim the word of God, the Holy Spirit shows up to empower.

Groups are made up of people who Jesus called with two simple words: "Follow me" (Matthew 4:19). Sometimes these people are like the apostle Peter, who despite his humble fisherman background and the failures he experienced in following Jesus, says in one of his letters to the churches that those who follow Jesus are "a chosen people, a royal priesthood, a holy nation, God's special possession" (1 Peter 2:9).

When these called out and chosen people pray for boldness to preach God's word and ask Him to do wonders, they can expect and believe God the Holy Spirit to fill them and work through them individually.

Now, Lord, look on their threats, and grant to Your servants that with all boldness they may speak Your word, by stretching out Your hand to heal, and that signs and wonders may be done through the name of Your holy Servant Jesus."

And when they had prayed, the place where they were assembled together was shaken; and they were all filled with the Holy Spirit, and they spoke the word of God with boldness. Acts 4:29-31 NKJV

CONCLUSION

This guide (and it is only a guide) will help your group or church to use the 5-step process to reach out to any One!

Whether you are using this alone or as part of a group God will help you to identify the One! to focus on over the next 4 weeks or so. With the dynamic help and power of the Holy Spirit, you can walk carefully through the 5-Steps with the singular goal, of bringing One!Name into an active living relationship with Jesus as savior and Lord.

I believe you and your group or church can adapt this guide to suit your peculiar situation. If God is in it, then it will succeed. So invite Him to lead the way.

Printable Tools

There are a number of printable and customizable tools that your group will find useful, Including the One!Life Wall poster and the One!Life card, which is a small 13cm x 11cm (top x side) card with the following details:

1. Space to write One!Name who a group member seeks to invite to know Jesus.

2. Space to write your name/the group member's name.

3. Space to write the date when One!Name attends a church service/special program.

4. Space for a commendation Tick.

The One!Life Wall poster has spaces to fix and stick completed One!Life cards as members of the group invite and succeed with God's help in bringing One!Name to church services and programs.

When the One!Life card has been fully completed, it can be stuck on the One!Life Wall poster by using rolled up sellotape at the back of the card to stick it to the wall poster. Post-it paper could also be used if that is easier to get.

Groups, and church units can challenge every member to take one card at a time and go through the 5-Steps until they stick their completed card on the One!Life wall poster. Group members who complete the steps within 4 weeks can start again with another card and another name.

Your groups and/or church can run the 5-Step cycle up to 6 times a year or more or less. The One!Life Wall posters can be reused during each cycle.

Connect & Join the movement.

To connect with us as we run our One! programs and get help to you run your own One! programs check out our page on www.OneName.Life and on Facebook at https://fb.me/OneName.Life

Join the community and share your experiences and testimonies. See what other groups are doing with One! and post your photos too.

PRINTABLE TOOLS

One!Life Handy Card

One!Life Wall Poster Pin-Up

One!Life 5-Step Guide

One!Life Card

One!Life Card

Write One!Name here

Write your name here

Date: One!Name attended service/program

TICK: God did it through you

`13cm

One!Life Card

Step 1 -One!Name...

Step 2 -One!Prayer. Pray these over One!Name

(i) Hebrew 4:16 Ask for Mercy & Grace

(ii) John 16:8-9 Ask for a conviction of sin of not believing in Jesus as savior

(iii) Luke 15:17-18 Ask the Holy Spirit to led and for a repentant heart & decision to go back to the Father.

Step 3 - One!Invite. Send out an invite to church service/Special program using -Social media/Text message/Phone call/YesHeIs Video

Step 4 - One!Soul. Go out and bring One!Name to experience Jesus at a service or program.

Step 5- One!Life. Help One!Name to Read the Bible, One Chapter-a-day every day using YouVersion, start praying with your bible open and fellowshipping with believers regularly.

11cm

One!Life Wall Poster

One!Life Wall Poster

113cm/226cm

One!Life 5-Step Guide

One!Life

STEP 1- One!Name: _____

It starts with one lost sheep .Prayerfully ask God to show you someone in need of Jesus. write out One!Name.

STEP 2- One!Prayer: Take time daily over the next 7 days to pray this three-layered prayer for One!Name;

a) Ask for God's Mercy and Grace for One!Name.................................

Hebrew 4:16 -Let us therefore come boldly unto the throne of grace, that we may obtain mercy, and find grace to help in time of need.

b) Ask the Holy Spirit to convict of sin.

John 16:8-9 And when He has come, He will convict the world of sin, and of righteousness, and of judgment: 9 of sin, because they do not believe in Me.

c) Ask for a repentant heart experience and the Spirit to prompt a return to God the Father.

Luke 15:17-18-17 "But when he came to himself, he said, 'How many of my father's hired servants have bread enough and to spare, and I perish with hunger! 18 I will arise and go to my father, and will say to him, "Father, I have sinned against heaven and before you.

STEP 3 - One!Invite -Send out an invitation to One!Name to attend a church service/an outreach program/mid-week service. Send out three types of invitation - a) Social media. A Direct message[Invite] on Facebook, Twitter, IG or other.

b) A text message/imessage/ email and

c) Make a phone call.

STEP 4- One!Soul -Go out and lovingly bring One!Name to service, a fun program or mid-week service. Pre-inform and come with One!Name to experience Jesus. Do this as many times as needed till One!Name accepts Jesus as savior and becomes a living soul.

STEP 5 - One!Life - Encourage & help One!Name to:

a) Start reading the bible One chapter a day (The book of John is a great place to start and YouVersion is a great App to get)

b) Pray daily from the word of God. Praying prayers from God's word with an open bible.

c) Fellowship regularly with a group of believers.

If your life is full of confusion and lots of things don't make sense and you feel lost, like a sheep that has gone astray and is wandering in a wild wasteland. If sin and negative habits get the better of you and you are bound by your sins.

I have great news for you, Jesus died to set you free from sin and was raised to give you a new heart and a new life in God.

Believe in God's gift of forgiveness and life through the death and resurrection of Jesus Christ and God's promise of salvation is yours.

God's word in Romans 10:9-10 NLT says "If you openly declare that Jesus is Lord and believe in your heart that God raised him from the dead, you will be saved. For it is by believing in your heart that you are made right with God, and it is by openly declaring your faith that you are saved."

You can say this prayer out loud right now;

Father, I believe you sent Jesus to pay for all of my sins so you could forgive me and give me a new start and a new life. I believe and confess that you raised Jesus from the dead to give me a new life in Jesus and that I am now made right with you because I believe. I invite you into my heart as Savior and ask you to teach me to make you Lord of my life. In Jesus Name I pray.

The word of God declares you are saved and have started a new life in Jesus today. Find a fellowship of believers so you can grow.

Made in the USA
Monee, IL
07 July 2026

56550207R00040